BELFAST FINDS LOG

Belfast Finds Log

Poems

For Maggie a Sea
with fondest love
Nigel

22·X·14

NIGEL PANTLING

Shoestring Press

ISBN 978-1-910323-06-9

ACKNOWLEDGEMENTS

With thanks to the editors of *The North, The Rialto*, and *Smiths Knoll*, where some of these poems first appeared.

Designed and typeset by Gerry Cambridge
gerry.cambridge@btinternet.com

Printed by Imprint Digital, Exeter
www.imprint.co.uk

Published by Shoestring Press
19, Devonshire Avenue, Beeston, Nottinghamshire, NG9 1BS
(0115) 925 1827
www.shoestringpress.co.uk

Contents

For my Parents

Parabola

Galileo defined the parabola as a curve
made of points equidistant from a line
and from a focus. He showed a projectile
falling under gravity followed a parabola.

Tonight's projectile is a tear gas canister
fired from the barrel of a self-loading rifle
from the cordon B Troop has formed
across Bligh's Lane, facing the barricade.

See how the canister arcs, rising to the
roof level of the houses opposite,
then reaching a high point, turns down,
as gravity pulls it back to earth.

Notice that when the canister breaks
the living room window of the house
it is at the same height as when launched.
For this parabola the directrix is the street

and the axis of symmetry is vertical.
The focus of the parabola is, as you see,
the family falling through their front door,
the tear-gas billowing behind them.

Duck Shooting on Clapham Common

That last day before Belfast,
after the dodgems and candy floss,
the coconut shy and hall of mirrors,
beyond the scarlet steam organ
wheezing *Waltzing Matilda*
we stopped at a rifle range—
six smiling metal ducks
tracking from left to right, then
one by one, diving from sight,
looping under, up and round again.

I paid my shilling, took the air-rifle,
pressed the stock into my shoulder,
aimed off for the bent fore-sight,
controlled my breathing,
eased the trigger
and knocked them down, all six,
toy tin duck by toy tin duck.

I turned to you and smiled.
When I looked back, my fallen ducks
had completed their hidden loop,
were upright, smiling, good as new.

Night Patrol

You're fed and briefed,
ready for the green snug
of the cap comforter,
the hug of the flak jacket
close under your arms
like the lift of your Dad's hands
when you were small.

You collect your rifle,
welcome the weight of it,
the warmth of the stock,
the rub of the sling
rough around your wrist.
You check for rattles, shines,
gaps in your cam cream,
make sure the wound dressing
is gaffer-taped to your belt.

Then a slap on the shoulder,
a laugh pitched a little high,
an obscenity for the duty officer
and you're on your way together
past the sentries, through the gates—
boy giants, owning the crepe black streets.

Instructions for Opening Fire

From the 'Yellow Card' issued to every soldier in Northern Ireland

Never use more force than the **minimum** necessary to enable you to carry out your duties.

At a road block, **you will NOT fire on a vehicle simply because it refuses to stop.**

Whenever possible a warning should be given before you open fire. A warning should be as loud as possible, preferably by loud-hailer.

If you have to challenge a person who is acting suspiciously you must do so in a firm, distinct, voice saying **"Halt— Hands Up"**.

If the person does not halt at once, you are to challenge again saying **"Halt—Hands Up"** and if the person does not halt on your second challenge you are to cock your weapon, apply the safety catch and shout: **"Stand still I am ready to fire"**.

You may fire after due warning against a person carrying what you can positively identify as a firearm, but only if you have reason to think he is about to use it for offensive purposes **and** he refuses to halt when called upon to do so, and there is no other way of stopping him.

You may fire after due warning against a person who, though he is not at present attacking has in your sight killed or seriously injured a member of the security forces or a person it is your duty to protect **and** not halted when called upon to do so and cannot be arrested by any other means.

You may fire without warning when hostile firing is taking place in your area and a warning is impracticable against a person using a firearm against you or those it is your duty to protect or against a person carrying what you can positively identify as a firearm if he is clearly about to use it for offensive purposes.

You may fire without warning if there is no other way to protect yourself or those whom it is your duty to protect from the danger of being killed or seriously injured.

Note: "Firearm" includes a grenade, nail bomb or gelignite type bomb.

Crossing Cromac Square

He's tail-end Charlie,
walking backward through The Lower Markets,
protecting his patrol from ambush from behind.

The Square—last year a sniper shot the back-marker here.
He covers as they crouch corner to corner,
doorway to doorway. He will be the last across.

He pulls the rifle harder into his shoulder,
interrogates roofs, doors, windows, alleyways.
He tests the safety catch with his thumb.

If he sees a target, he can aim and fire in a second.
An armalite round would cross the Square in half that.
He knows he would not hear the shot.

Test

By the time we reach the Ardoyne,
Greenidge has his century
and England are coming out to face
Roberts and Holding at their fastest.

Our orders are to hold the line
by a show of armed force,
to do nothing aggressive,
staying put as long as we can.

There are only eight of us.
The crowd can see that
and they're running,
scooping stones, bricks, bottles.

Back at Old Trafford,
Edrich and Close
ducking what they can
are taking hits to the body.

Londonderry, August 1971

He thinks of his parents tonight
drinking tea by the gas fire, listening
to the latest goings-on in Ambridge.

The firelight here is at the barricades
where petrol bombs arc overhead,
smashing to spatter glass and flame.

He can hear only the clang, clang, clang
of dustbin lids, the crowd's raw throat,
the crack of baton rounds, the pain.

After the Riot

At last we're on our way back to base,
and we've come via Stranmillis: as we roll
through the gates of the Botanic Gardens,
past the stove wing of the Palm House,
frangipani stains the evening with peaches
and the scarlet spikes of the bromeliads
press against the glass to wave us by.

Headlights off, gearbox in neutral,
and we're letting gravity take the strain,
pulling us down the long slope to the Lagan.
We coast in the quarter-moon darkness,
soothed by the white noise of the tyres,
glad of the chance to greet old friends.

On we slide, past oaks, ash, hornbeam,
the familiar stands of Persimmon,
Tulip Tree, Lebanese Cedar,
until we reach the Ginkgo Biloba:
a native of China and Japan,
a species with no living relative,
unchanged since the Pliocene.

First Contact

Shout—house with green door ground floor window lone gunman
    follow me now
Radio—made contact gunman Stratheden Street section in hot
    pursuit

de-bus
shoulder door
smell cordite
check front room
—clear—
send two men
upstairs
room by room
— all clear—
along hall
kitchen
—clear—
back door ajar
into yard
kick open sheds
—all clear—
nothing.

Regroup by the gate to the alley, recover breath, remember
the thin toy crack of the armalite, bullets drilling past

open gate
check left, right
cross alley
put boots to

gate opposite
cross yard
into house
old couple
in armchairs
mouths open
straight through
out onto
Spamount Street
no-one about
no traffic
no kids
nothing
nothing
nothing

Fall back to the vehicle, inspect the holes in the canopy,
argue over who came closest, laugh at the novelty of it.

Car Insurance

He's driving the white civilian mini,
mud-splashed and a dented bumper,
the number plates changed last week.
He's wearing T-shirt and flares,
his hair's as long as it's ever been
and his sideburns reach his chin.
He's sure he'll pass for a local
so long as he doesn't open his mouth.
There should be no problem this trip—
up the Falls Road and on to Lisburn,
hand over the weekly report, cup of tea
and safely back to base by nightfall.
His insurance is under the passenger seat,
a Browning, with a round in the chamber.

Vehicle Patrol

It was an ordinary van, Belfast City Laundry
painted on its side, parked in a side street.
Ordinary, although now you mention it,
heavy on its springs, the door taped shut.

Anyway, there was room to pull in behind
for a smoke-break. They stopped there—
helmets off, rifles resting across their knees—
for ten minutes. Ten minutes, the time

it takes a soldier to crack a few jokes,
finish a cigarette. Also the time
to run a clock down to zero,
to trip a rocker switch, to fire a detonator.

Stop and Search

They are blocking the road on Brompton Park again,
searching the cars as they leave the Ardoyne Club.
They stop him as they have a hundred times.

He knows them all by sight: the studiedly polite boys;
the surly ones, resenting being back in the Six Counties;
the slapdash; the old hands, crafty with the rifle butt.

Today it is the sergeant who orders him from the car,
checks under the seats, in the pockets of the doors.
He says nothing, keeps his eyes on the pavement.

The sergeant tells him to open the boot.
When the lid has them covered, he passes across
a folded paper: a name, an address, a hiding place.

Covert Observation

A street light stutters,
then blackness.
Not black enough though
to stop the shadows
slithering at the windows
of his hiding place.
In his ear, the hooves
of his own heartbeat.
Somewhere close by
movement, voices,
fingers pointing.
He remembers being six,
how it felt to be alone.

Radio Silence

Hello All Stations, this is Two One. Send sitrep when in position.
Out.

Hello Two One, this is Two One Alpha.
In position, all quiet. Over.

Two One, Roger. Out.

Hello Two One, this is Two One Charlie.
In position, all quiet. Over.

Two One, Roger. Out.

Hello Two One, this is Two One Bravo.
In position, all quiet. Over.

Two One, what took you so long? Over.

Two One Bravo, we had to wait for the pub to empty
before we could get into the back of the building. Over.

Charlie, more likely they had a quick one on the way upstairs.

Alpha, I hope you're bringing some booze back
for the rest of us, we're going to need it after this fucking caper.

Bravo, in your fucking dreams, son.

Charlie, at least you're not up to your neck in fucking ditch water.

Alpha, my heart bleeds, I'm up a fucking tree and it's pissing down.

Bravo, fat chance we have of a catch here, any sensible fucking Provo is tucked up in bed.

Charlie, yeah, with your fucking wife.

Alpha, you haven't seen his fucking wife.

Bravo, anybody says that about my fucking wife, they got me to answer to.

Charlie, yeah? You and whose fucking army?

Hello all stations this is Two One. Anything happening? Over.

Two One Alpha, negative. All quiet. Out.

Two One Bravo, no. All quiet. Out

Two One Charlie, all quiet. Out.

R and R in Liverpool

Seagulls cart-wheel in the sunlight
as she meets the Belfast ferry.
He arrives mute, hunched, hooded.

Too early for the hotel,
she shows him the Walker:
Guercino's reclining nude,

her curtain lifted like a veil.
He scans the pedimenti
for signs of movement.

Over dinner, he talks about stags,
sangars, sunray, felix and goliath,
radio call-signs and radio silence.

Belfast Finds Log: 24 January 1975

Armalite with 14 rounds, plus a Smith and Wesson
under the floorboards, derelict house, Lower Markets.

Browning pistol (army issue—serial number gone)
behind a loose brick, eight feet up, the bakery Newtonards.

Martini Henry, Boer-War vintage, could still be fired
wrapped in canvas waterproofing, drainage ditch, Dunmurray.

M1 Carbine, assorted ammo (none for an M1)
in roof space of outhouse, Ardoyne back-to-back.

1500 miscellaneous cartridges
found by search dog at New Lodge road block.

Eight electric timing circuits, minus detonators
in shoe box on wardrobe in the Divis Flats.

Fifty sticks commercial explosive, mostly weeping
in City Centre dustbin, following tip-off.

Sterling SMG and shot gun, berets, arm-bands, flags
behind bar at the Old King James on Shankhill Road.

Two point 22 air pistols with four pipe bombs (primed)
in drain below manhole in Short Strand lock-up.

AK 47 rifle, barrel warm and smelling of cordite
under female baby in pram, on the Falls Road.

In the Interrogation Centre

Hearing a sound out of place, I open the door.
A boy in jeans and Wolfe Tone T-shirt
leans bleeding against the cell wall.
He stares at me across four hundred years.

My sergeant, arm still raised,
turns his head. His eyes say
'Mind your own fucking business, Sir.
I know these people better than you'.

The ceiling lights pin three shadows
to the ripples of the concrete floor.
Sweat glitters on our faces.
The only noise, our breathing.

Shoppers

While they're queuing at your gate, you hear
'another soldier dead in Derry'
'Sean's gone on the blanket in the Kesh'
'the Boys have shot a tout in Omagh'.

After the search and the bag check,
when they're off down Donegall Street,
it's Christmas this and Christmas that,
and 'what shall we get for the wee girls?'

A Wager with Special Branch

'Find McGuigan and I'll buy you a whiskey'.
Not much of a wager, but that's Special Branch,
always making out his workload is so tough
no blow-in from England could be in the picture.
I wasn't going to let him make me feel small.
I said, make it a case, and Bushmills (it's the best).

McGuigan: reckoned to be the Belfast Brigade's best
quartermaster. He'd stashed loaded pistols in whiskey
barrels, hidden twenty detonator leads in one small
bush, winding individual wires round each branch.
We knew he was short: five foot one, but no picture
of him anywhere in our files—this would be tough.

I geed up my intelligence section, talking tough,
said to turn over the houses McGuigan knew best,
to look for a picture of him, any fucking picture.
Told them our reputation as well as a case of whiskey
was at stake. Said search his family home, then branch
out, search the houses he'd lived in when he was small.

We found an old passport photograph—very small
but better than nothing—at fifteen: he looked tough
even then. I blew it up, showed it to Special Branch,
who shrugged, but you could tell it was easily the best
lead to date. We'd arrested four men drinking whiskey
with a woman in an illegal club, you get the picture:

I checked each of the men against McGuigan's picture.
It was no good: any likeness was too small,
and they were all six foot. They breathed whiskey

over me and sneered. I knew that I had to tough
this out, pretend it didn't matter, it was all for the best.
I wanted to save face in front of Special Branch—

you have to save face in front of Special Branch.
Suddenly he stopped laughing. His face was a picture:
the penny had dropped that I'd come off best.
The woman we'd got didn't look small
but wearing six inch heels must have been tough
for a man, and that wig! I could taste my whiskey.

Special Branch scowled, tapped the grip of his small-
arm, suggested I see the bigger picture. I'm not tough:
I said perhaps after all it was best he keep the whiskey.

No Surrender

She is ironing his white shirt,
the one he left crumpled
on the bathroom floor.

She fastens the buttons,
presses a crease in the sleeves,
carries it upstairs on a hanger,
hooks it behind his bedroom door.

Next week she will take it down,
wash it with her blouses, rinse,
spin, tumble and iron it once again.

She always has it ready, this white shirt,
though it's worn paper thin
and frayed at collar and cuff
from washing every week since.

Training Officer

He taught them to know the M1 carbine
from the Armalite, making them shout
the name of each as they heard it fired.
He showed them how to spot a sniper
by ignoring the crack of the bullet
and looking to the thump of the rifle
for a door edging shut, a curtain shivering.
They learned the pop of a mortar,
the flaming track of the petrol bomb,
the rattle of the rolling nail bomb.
They smelt the marzipan of
home-made explosive and
moulded Semtex with bare hands.

Now, four months later, they are back,
bubbling with stories of dawn raids,
of gun-men arrested in bed with girls,
weapons hidden below floors, in walls,
car bombs found with the timer stopped
or the detonator loose, and laughing
about guns fired from churches or cars,
bullets that missed by the distance you travel
in a Landover in a quarter of a second,
cheese-wire across the road at neck height
snagging and cutting the vehicle just in front,
and only one of them dead, just one, just one dead.
He laughs with them then, pats backs, breathes out.

17th September 1984

This morning, in Balham, Bristol, Birmingham,
men who were soldiers in the Seventies
go about their civilian business.

This morning, in room 629 in Brighton,
a visitor who has registered as Roy Walsh
draws six Phillips screws from a bath panel
deposits twenty pounds of Frangex, a detonator,
and a timer made from a video recorder.

This morning, in Belfast,
an active service unit commander
waits beside a phone for a codeword.

Photograph Album

His daughter has found the album
tucked in the spare room cupboard.
She brings it to him, flipping the pages,
calling him from his reading and music.

She asks him who they are,
these young men holding
boards across their chests,
chalked with names and dates.

He explains: officer commanding,
quartermaster, adjutant, volunteer.
'And the dates, Dad?'
That was when he had them interned.

She asks how that makes him feel.
He says that it was his job in those days
to find these men and lock them up.
'Yes, Dad, but how does that make you feel?'

Back in Tesco's

'Will you need help packing, Sir?'
He stares at the girl, at his empty hands,
at the conveyer belt where his groceries
have unloaded themselves in their habitual order—
non-perishables, chilled and frozen,
vegetables, fruit—and at the back
the plums, black as blood.